SKIN

by Eric Geron

Children's Press®
An imprint of Scholastic Inc.

Library of Congress Cataloging-in-Publication Data

Names: Geron, Eric, author.
Title: Skin / by Eric Geron.
Description: First edition. | New York : Children's Press, an imprint of
    Scholastic Inc., 2024. | Series: Learn about: animal coverings |
    Includes index. | Audience: Ages 5–7. | Audience: Grades K–1. | Summary:
    "Let's learn all about the different types of animal coverings! Animals
    have different body coverings for different reasons. Some animals use
    their coverings to keep warm or stay cool, others use them for
    protection, and can either stand out or blend in. Some animals even use
    their coverings to move! This vibrant new set of LEARN ABOUT books gives
    readers a close-up look at five different animal coverings, from fur and
    feathers to skin, scales, and shells. Each book is packed with
    photographs and fun facts that explore how each covering suits the
    habitat, diet, survival, and life cycle of various animals in the
    natural world. Frogs, salamanders, and humans are covered in skin.
    Actually, did you know that every animal with a backbone has some type
    of skin covering its body? Discover all the incredible ways that skin
    helps animals survive. With amazing photos and lively text, this book
    explains how skin helps animals stay dry, keep warm, protect themselves,
    breathe, and more! Get ready to learn all about skin!"—Provided by
    publisher.
Identifiers: LCCN 2023000183 (print) | LCCN 2023000184 (ebook) |
    ISBN 9781338898118 (library binding) | ISBN 9781338898125 (paperback) |
    ISBN 9781338898132 (ebk)
Subjects: LCSH: Skin—Juvenile literature. | Body covering
    (Anatomy)—Juvenile literature. | Animals—Adaptations—Juvenile
    literature. | BISAC: JUVENILE NONFICTION / Animals / General | JUVENILE
    NONFICTION / Science & Nature / General (see also headings under Animals
    or Technology)
Classification: LCC QL941 .G47 2024 (print) | LCC QL941 (ebook) | DDC
    591.47—dc23/eng/20230110
LC record available at https://lccn.loc.gov/2023000183
LC ebook record available at https://lccn.loc.gov/2023000184

10 9 8 7 6 5 4 3 2 1   24 25 26 27 28
Printed in China   62

First edition, 2024
Book design by Kay Petronio

Photos ©: 7 top left: SteveByland/Getty Images; 7
bottom left: Baroness/500px/Getty Images; 9 top right:
Supersmario/Getty Images; 18 main: Mlenny/Getty Images;
19: Hoberman Collection/Universal Images Group/Getty
Images; 21 inset: davemhuntphotography/Getty Images;
22 inset: Courtesy of the Dallas Zoo; 24: JasonOndreicka/
Getty Images; 29 center right: Mark Kostich/Getty Images.

All other photos © Shutterstock.

A special thank-you
to the team at the
Cincinnati Zoo &
Botanical Garden
for their expert
consultation.

CONTENTS

Introduction: Skin-Deep 4

Chapter 1: Special Skin 8

Chapter 2: Saved by Skin 12

Chapter 3: Thick and Thin Skin 16

Chapter 4: Hide-and-Skin 20

Chapter 5: What Else Can Skin Do? 24

Conclusion: Skin Matters 30

Glossary 31

Index/About the Author 32

Skin-Deep

Animal bodies can have different coverings. Some are covered with fur or feathers. Others are covered with shells or scales. Some animals have more than one covering! This book is all about a special covering: skin! Skin can be spotted or striped, thick or thin, and wrinkly or smooth.

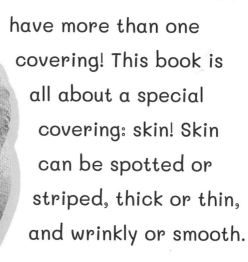

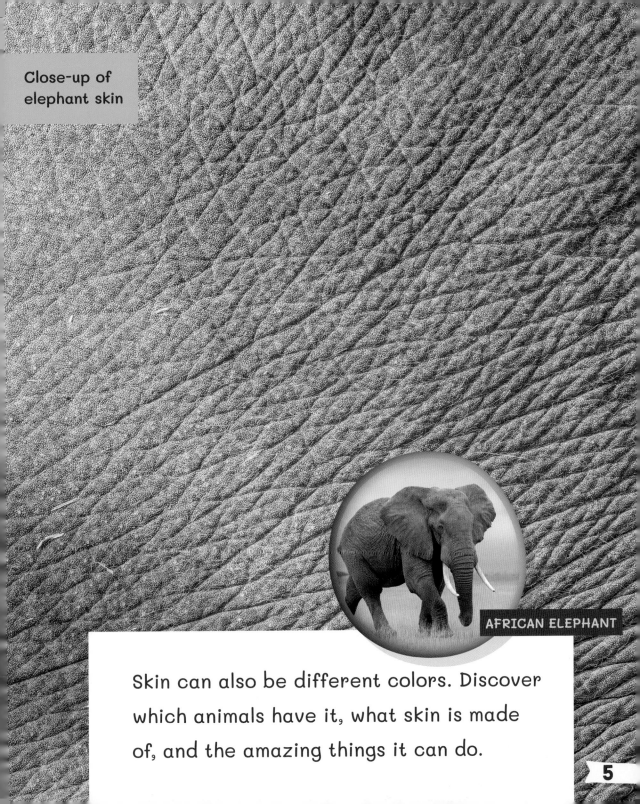

Close-up of
elephant skin

AFRICAN ELEPHANT

Skin can also be different colors. Discover which animals have it, what skin is made of, and the amazing things it can do.

Which Animals Have Skin?

Reptiles, **mammals**, **amphibians**, and birds have skin! These animals have **backbones** and breathe air. Some live on land and some live in water.

Did you know humans are mammals?

Mammals and birds are **warm-blooded** animals. Amphibians, fish, and reptiles are **cold-blooded** animals.

CHAPTER 1

Special Skin

Skin is really useful for animals. Just like there are different types of animals, there are also different types of skin. Each type of skin plays an important role. Some skin protects against water loss and helps an animal keep warm or stay cool.

AFRICAN CROWNED CRANE

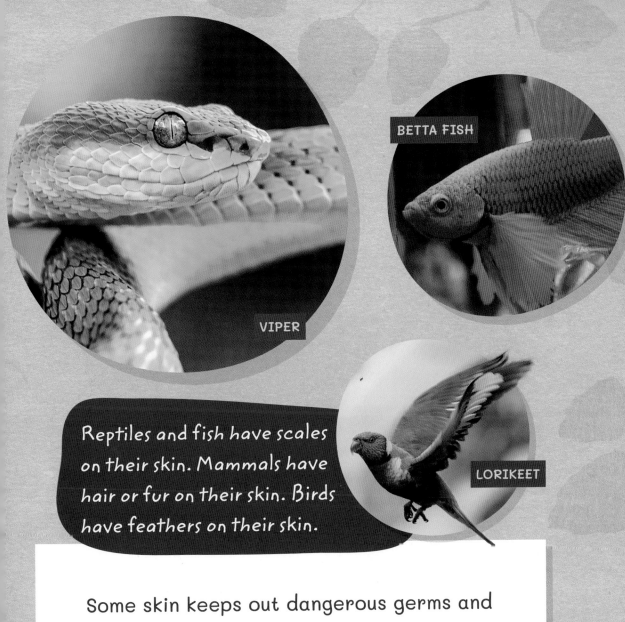

BETTA FISH

VIPER

LORIKEET

Reptiles and fish have scales on their skin. Mammals have hair or fur on their skin. Birds have feathers on their skin.

Some skin keeps out dangerous germs and diseases. Some skin hides an animal from **predators** or **prey**. Skin gives animals the sense of touch and lets them feel things like temperature and pressure.

SPHYNX CAT

Skin

This is a sphynx cat. It is a mammal. Its smooth skin barely has any hair.

Mammal skin has different layers. The epidermis, or top layer, gives skin its color and protects the body from the weather.

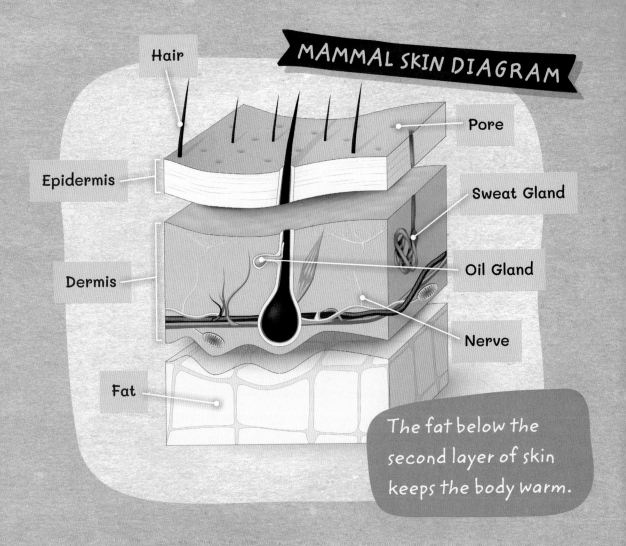

Hair

Pore

Epidermis

Sweat Gland

Oil Gland

Dermis

Nerve

Fat

The fat below the second layer of skin keeps the body warm.

The dermis, or second layer of skin, has nerve endings. These tell the brain about sensations including heat, cold, and pain. It also has glands that release sweat and oil through tiny holes called **pores**.

CHAPTER 2

Saved by Skin

Skin protects animals in many ways! It holds the body together and keeps different organs inside it. Without skin, those body parts could easily get damaged.

MANATEE

If the skin on a mammal has a deep cut, the body can close it up. This is how a scar is made!

AKHAL-TEKE HORSE

Skin allows animals to feel if something is harmful. It lets the brain know how to react. Skin also acts as a shield to protect animals against harmful germs getting into their bodies.

Skintight

Skin can protect the bodies of animals from soaking up water. Sweat and oils act like a natural protective coating over a mammal's skin. Some birds create oils that coat their skin and feathers in a waterproof covering.

BLUE JAYS

Some reptiles use their scaly skin to hold in water. This lets them live on land where it can be very dry and hot. Amphibians can use their skin to drink water!

Amphibian skin is moist and slimy.

CHAPTER 3

Thick and Thin Skin

Animals use their skin to help control their body temperature. One way an animal can keep warm is by having thick skin to trap heat close to its body. The polar bear has thick skin under its fur that allows it to keep warm in the cold.

You may think the skin of a fluffy white polar bear is white, but it is actually black!

MONITOR LIZARD

Reptiles and amphibians use their skin to soak up heat from the sun and raise their body temperatures. Sometimes, they can absorb the heat from rocks warmed by the sun.

Cooling Down

A lot of animals use their skin to keep cool. Skin can protect animals from the heat. The thick skin on the knees and chest of a camel allows it to sit on the hot desert sand without getting burned.

CAMEL

Did you know that elephants have wrinkly skin to keep cool? After a bath or rainstorm, their wrinkles store the water for the next hot day!

ASIAN ELEPHANT

RHINOS

Rhinos roll in mud to coat their thick skin. This keeps them from getting sunburned. Birds and reptiles can go in the shade to avoid getting overheated. Amphibians' skin soaks up water to keep from drying out. Water exits their skin to help them cool off.

CHAPTER 4

Hide-and-Skin

Many reptiles and amphibians have skin that allows them to hide in their **habitat**. The ability to blend into their surroundings is called **camouflage**. Camouflage helps protect animals from being seen by predators or prey.

Reptile skin is dry and scaly.

TOKAY GECKO

MOSSY FROG

MOORISH GECKO

The mossy frog vanishes into its background because its bumpy skin looks like moss. The Moorish gecko's skin can change colors. Its skin can match the color of the surface beneath it to seem out of sight.

21

Skin-Visible

The skin of fish, birds, and some mammals can also blend in with their habitat. Having dark skin allows certain fish that are deep in the sea to hide. Beluga whales are white to trick hungry predators into thinking they are chunks of ice.

Did you know that tigers have striped fur and striped skin?

Close-up of tiger skin

TIGER

Snow leopards and tigers use the patterns on their skin and fur to camouflage. The animals blend into the shadows cast by trees in the daytime.

CHAPTER 5

What Else Can Skin Do?

Animals can also use their skin to feel what is going on around them. Some animals even use their skin to breathe! Mammals and birds mainly breathe in air through their nose and mouth (or beak for birds).

The lungless salamander only breathes through its skin.

AXOLOTL

Some amphibians and fish breathe in oxygen from the water. They create **mucus** that coats their bodies. This mucus helps them breathe by allowing water to pass through their skin.

Skin Protection

The colors of skin protect animals from predators by warning them to back off. Most of the time, colorful skin lets predators know their prey will not taste good. Brightly colored skin can tip predators off that an animal is poisonous.

FIRE-BELLIED TOAD

The most deadly amphibian is the golden poison dart frog.

SCORPIONFISH

Certain types of fish ooze poison out of their skin, like the scorpionfish and spotted trunkfish. The electric eel has skin that can shock its prey!

Second Skin

Many animals lose a layer of skin and replace it with a healthy new one. This is called **molting**, or shedding. As the reptile or amphibian grows, it molts pieces of old skin for new ones. This way the skin can grow with the rest of the body.

Molting chameleon

Fish do not molt. Their scaly skin grows with them.

Gecko

Boa

Cardinal

Some mammals shed skin and fur to keep themselves free of pests. Mammals shed skin over time. Most reptiles and amphibians shed their outer layer of skin all at once. Birds shed their feathers over time or all at once.

CONCLUSION

CAMEL

Skin Matters

Now you know all about skin! It can be dry and scaly or moist and smooth. Skin helps animals control their temperature and keep their organs safe. It also helps animals hide from view, protect themselves against predators, and in some cases, breathe. Next time you see an animal covered in skin, remember all the amazing things its skin can do!

The animal with the toughest skin in the world is the crocodile!

GLOSSARY

amphibian (am-FIB-ee-uhn) a cold-blooded animal with a backbone that lives in water and breathes with gills when young; as an adult, it develops lungs and lives on land

backbone (BAK-bohn) a set of connected bones that runs down the middle of the back; also called the spine

camouflage (KAM-uh-flahzh) a disguise or natural coloring that allows animals to hide by making them look like their surroundings

cold-blooded (KOHLD bluhd-id) having a body temperature that changes according to the temperature of the surroundings, like reptiles and fish

habitat (HAB-i-tat) the place where an animal or plant is usually found

mammal (MAM-uhl) a warm-blooded animal that has hair or fur and usually gives birth to live babies

molt (mohlt) to lose old fur, feathers, shell, or skin so that a new layer can grow

mucus (MYOO-kuhs) a thick, slimy liquid that coats and protects the inside or outside of an animal's body

pore (por) one of the tiny holes in an animal's skin that releases sweat and oil

predator (PRED-uh-tur) an animal that lives by hunting other animals for food

prey (pray) an animal that is hunted by another animal for food

reptile (REP-tile) a cold-blooded animal that crawls across the ground or creeps on short legs; most reptiles have backbones and lay eggs

warm-blooded (WORM bluhd-id) having a body temperature that does not change, even if the temperature of the surroundings is very hot or very cold

INDEX

A

amphibians, 6—7
amphibian skin, 15, 17, 19—21, 28—29

B

birds, 6—7, 9
bird skin, 9, 14, 29
blending in, 20—23

C

camouflage, 20—23

F

feeling through skin, 11, 13, 24
fish, 7
fish skin, 9, 22, 27, 28

H

hiding, 20—23

L

layers of mammal skin, 10—11

M

mammals, 6—7
mammal skin, 9—11, 12, 14, 22—23, 29

R

reptiles, 6—7
reptile skin, 9, 15, 17, 20, 28—29

S

scales, 9, 28
shedding, 28—29
skin. *See also* amphibian skin; bird skin; fish skin; mammal skin; reptile skin

about, 4—5, 8—11, 30
breathing through, 24—25
colors and patterns, 16, 22, 26
functions of, 12—27
losing and replacing, 28—29
protection, 19, 26—27
thick and thin, 16—19, 30
types of, 8—11
water and, 14—15, 25

T

temperature control, 16—19

W

wrinkles, 18

ABOUT THE AUTHOR

Eric Geron is the author of many books. He lives in New York City with his tiny dog, whose skin is covered in a fluffy white coat.